BEYOND THE THEORY: SCIENCE OF THE FUTURE

WILL ROBOTS EVER BE SMARTER THAN HUMANS?

THEORIES ABOUT ARTIFICIAL INTELLIGENCE

Tom Jackson

Gareth Stevens PUBLISHING

Please visit our website, www.garethstevens.com.
For a free color catalog of all our high-quality books,
call toll free 1-800-542-2595 or fax 1-877-542-2596.

Cataloging-in-Publication Data

Names: Jackson, Tom.
Title: Will robots ever be smarter than humans? theories about artificial intelligence / Tom Jackson.
Description: New York : Gareth Stevens Publishing, 2019. | Series: Beyond the theory: science of the future | Includes glossary and index.
Identifiers: LCCN ISBN 9781538226599 (pbk.) | ISBN 9781538226582 (library bound)
Subjects: LCSH: Artificial intelligence--Juvenile literature. | Technological innovations--Juvenile literature. | Conscious automata--Juvenile literature.
Classification: LCC Q335.4 J33 2019 | DDC 006.3--dc23

First Edition

Published in 2019 by
Gareth Stevens Publishing
111 East 14th Street, Suite 349
New York, NY 10003

Produced for Gareth Stevens by Calcium
Editors: Sarah Eason and Tim Cooke
Designers: Emma DeBanks and Lynne Lennon
Picture researcher: Rachel Blount

Picture credits: Cover: Shutterstock: Esin Deniz: background, Phonlamai Photo: foreground; Inside: Shutterstock: Andrey_Popov: p. 20; Andrew Angelov: p. 24; Basel101658: p. 27t; Bilanol: p. 32; Dmytro Bochkov: p. 36; Breakermaximus: p. 41; Cafe Racer: p. 31; Diabluses: p. 19; Freedomz: p. 28; Gyn9037: p. 34; Herrndorff: p. 22; lenetstan: p. 37; Indiphoto: p. 4; Lenscap Photography: p. 25; Maxx-Studio: p. 42; Titima Ongkantong: p. 12; Phonlamai Photo: pp. 5, 39; PhuShutter: p. 21; Pinglabel: p. 13; Prostock-studio: pp. 14, 17; Roka: p. 23; Samuray Studio: p. 26; Ampol Sandee: p. 16; Sl_photo: p. 15; Sergey Tarasov: pp. 1, 38; Vs148: p. 18; Zapp2Photo: p. 33; Wikimedia Commons: Matthew Breindel: p. 27b; Sue Clark: p. 6; D-Wave Systems, Inc.: p. 43; Daderot: p. 8; DARPA: p. 40; Raysonho @ Open Grid Scheduler / Grid Engine: p. 29; Adam Schuster: p. 11; Sunfox: p. 10; UL Digital Library: p. 35; U.S. Air Force photo/Bobbi Zapka: p. 30; U.S. Lithograph Co.: p. 9; Marcin Wicha: p. 7.

Printed in the United States of America

CPSIA compliance information: Batch #CS18GS:
For further information contact Gareth Stevens, New York, New York at 1-800-542-2595.

CONTENTS

-CHAPTER 1-

-CHAPTER 2-

-CHAPTER 3-

-CHAPTER 4-

-CHAPTER 5-

-CHAPTER 6-

WHAT IS A ROBOT?

Everyone is familiar with the idea of a robot, but precisely what a robot is can be difficult to define. On one level, a robot is any machine that is designed to perform a task automatically. In this definition, a vending machine dispensing candy, hot drinks, or soda is a robot. However, most people agree that robots are "smart" devices that have the ability to act a little more like humans. In contrast, a drink machine is simple. Robots do not have to look like humans, but robot engineering—known as robotics—is often inspired by natural forms. There are worm robots, fish robots, and dog robots. Humanlike machines, which have a head, eyes, hands, and legs, are called androids. However, robots do not even need a physical body. A "bot" is a computer program that does online jobs automatically.

When you select a hot drink or a soda from a vending machine, you are operating a robot.

Whatever they look like, robots have three main **components**: **sensors**, **processors**, and **effectors**. Sensors collect input, or information. They range from cameras or microphones to—in a drink machine—a button that selects a drink. An effector is the robot's output system. It could be a robotic arm or a human voice—or it could be a nozzle that squirts coffee into cups. Processors turn inputs into output. The processor of the drink machine has a simple task: it selects the correct drink. A more advanced robot has more complex tasks. For that the processor needs **artificial intelligence** (AI).

An AI is a machine that can make decisions. To make an AI that matches an EI—"evolved intelligence," like our own—we first have to understand what makes us smart in the first place. To find out how AI might reproduce human intelligence, we have to go beyond the theory.

We often imagine robots as machines that think in the same way as humans.

MECHANICAL SERVANTS

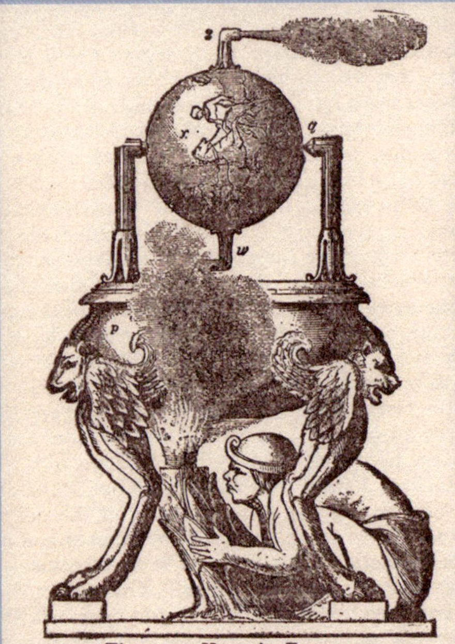

Fig. 21 —Heron's Eolipile.

This illustration shows the steam engine designed by Heron in ancient Greece.

Some early robots appeared in 1921 in a play by the Czech writer Karel Capek. Capek's play was about a world in which artificial humans were made in factories. In the play, these robots are built to serve humans. Instead (spoiler alert!), they end up rebelling against their masters and wiping out the human race!

People's fear of robots has never gone away. Leading scientists still worry today about the threat AI might pose to humanity. Despite this, robotics engineers have worked over the last century to make Capek's ideas a reality. The idea of having machines to do all our work for us is as appealing as the idea of machines taking over is terrifying.

Inventors have been dreaming up **mechanical** servants for centuries. In the first century AD, the Greek engineer Heron, who lived in Alexandria, Egypt, built what is now regarded as the first steam engine, the aeopile or "wind gate." The machine used jets of hot steam to create a spinning action. Heron did not use the aeopile to do any tasks, but he did design a workshop where everything was powered by steam—including the robot metalworkers.

UNANSWERED

Machines that operate independently are called **automata**. They are designed to repeat a set of instructions. However, Karel Capek named the mechanical characters in his play *robota*, based on the Hungarian word for "slave." Capek's new word was translated into English as robot. Today, it describes a machine that can be **programmed** to carry out a complex task or tasks. However, will the robots of the future be slaves? Or will they be the masters?

In 1495, the Italian artist and inventor Leonardo Da Vinci designed a metal man moved by a series of gears and levers. By the eighteenth century, clockwork devices called automata were amazing people across Europe. These automata were little more than complex toys. Some could draw and write, for example, but they always repeated the same pictures and words. The Turk seemed to be different. This chess-playing automaton could beat any human opponent, using an elaborate mechanism that whirred and clicked. However, it was eventually revealed that a very small chess expert was hidden inside! The dream of truly mechanical servants would have to wait for twentieth-century technology to make them real.

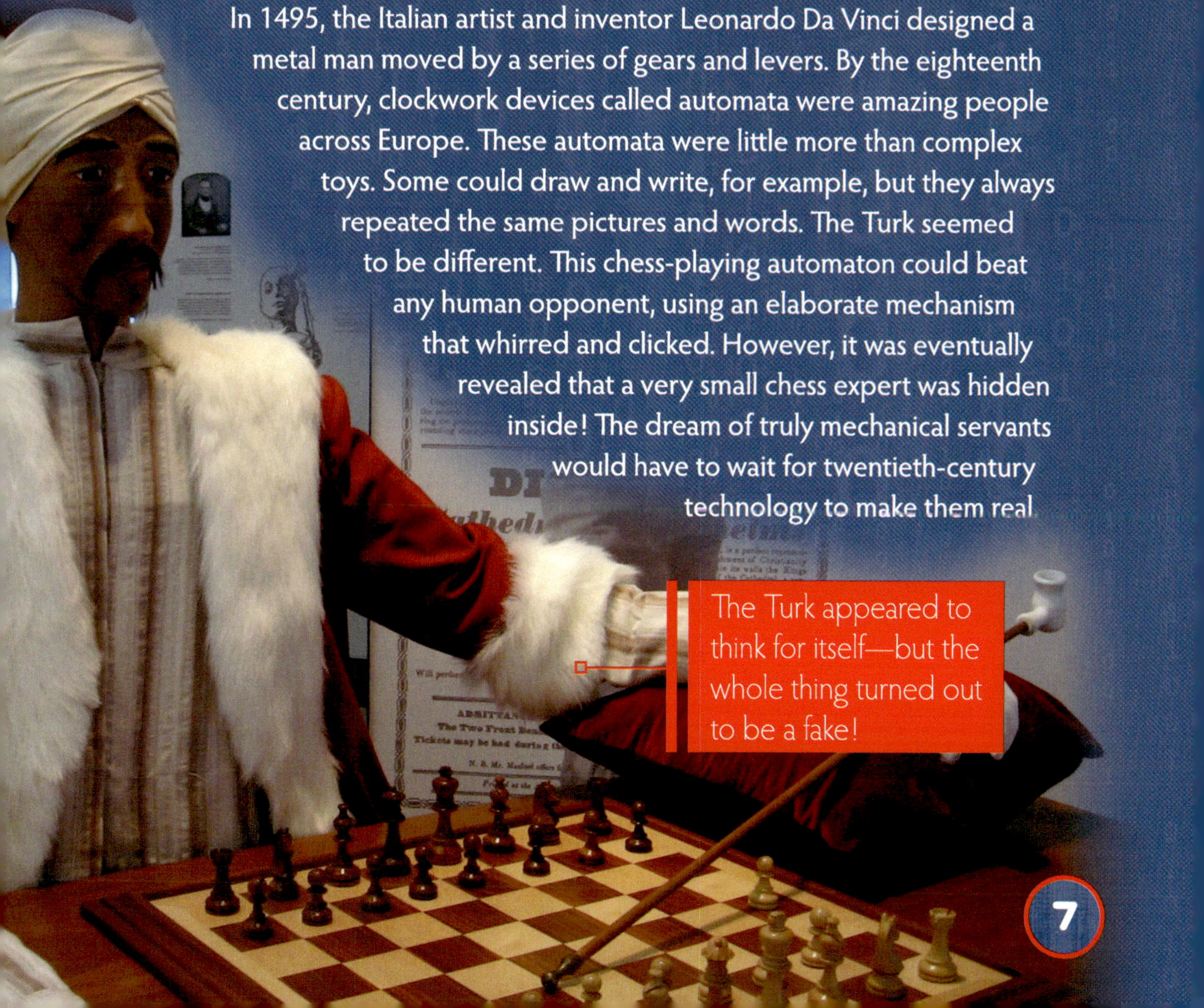

The Turk appeared to think for itself—but the whole thing turned out to be a fake!

THE FIRST ROBOTS

The first modern robots appeared in the late 1920s. However, these "mechanical men" were not built to perform practical tasks. They were designed to show off the skills of engineering companies. The robots used a wealth of new inventions. For example, radio technology had just been invented, so designers used it to control robots remotely. Early robots also used many electromechanical devices, in which magnetically controlled switches turned different components on and off. The robots' motion was provided by electric motors, which were small but still powerful. The motors were driven by a single power source, usually a battery inside the robot.

The US android Elektro had his own robot dog, named Sparko.

One of the most famous early robots was Erik, a British android designed in 1928. It could sit down and stand up again, and transmit a voice received by radio. Ten years later the US company Westinghouse built Elektro, a voice-controlled 6.5-foot-tall (2 m) android that could walk, blow up balloons, and smoke cigarettes!

BEHIND THE THEORY

Many of the ideas behind robotics originally came from science fiction, or futuristic stories based on scientific ideas. They included Capek's robota, the Tin Man from *The Wizard of Oz* (1900), and Maria, a robot character from the futuristic 1927 movie *Metropolis*. The person often called the "father of robotics" was the Russian American author Isaac Asimov. Asimov wrote dozens of science fiction stories that imagined a world with advanced technology.

In the 1940s, the writer Isaac Asimov came up with the Three Laws of Robotics. He designed them to ensure that robots would never take over humans:

1. A robot may not injure a human being or, through inaction, allow a human being to come to harm.
2. A robot must obey the orders given it by human beings, except where such orders would conflict with the First Law.
3. A robot must protect its own existence as long as such protection does not conflict with the First or Second Laws.

One early imagined robot was the Tin Man from *The Wizard of Oz* stories.

TAKING INSTRUCTIONS

A robot's hardware—its motors, sensors, and effectors—function automatically due to its software, or programming. A program is a list of instructions. The instructions have to be ordered in such a way that the robot "knows" how to turn one of several inputs from the sensors into the correct outputs produced by the effectors.

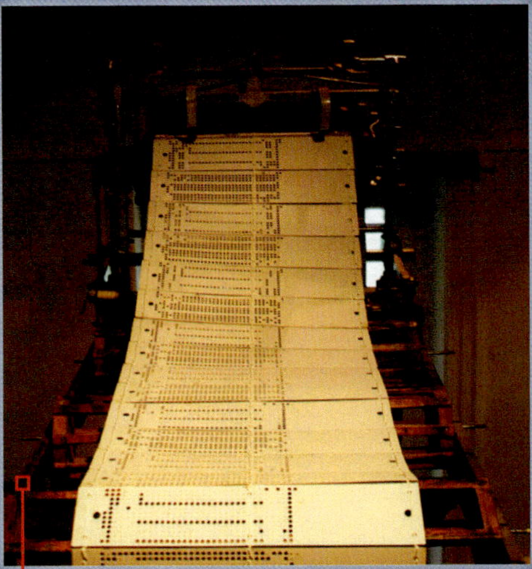

Holes in a series of punched cards are used to program a **loom** to weave patterns.

Some tasks that are simple for humans, such as putting an object into a box, require complex programming. The program has to account for every step in the process. (By contrast, some tasks that humans find difficult, such as performing complex math, are easy to program.) Some types of AI programs are attempting to make robots figure out the required steps for themselves. That would mean they were able to learn new tasks without the need for a human programmer.

The first programs were stored as holes punched into cards. These punched cards were first used in 1804 by a French merchant named Joseph Marie Charles to **automate** a loom that wove patterns in cloth. The holes corresponded to the position of a particular color of thread.

BEHIND THE THEORY

The first computer programmer was Ada Lovelace, daughter of the English poet Lord Byron. In the 1840s, Lovelace worked with Charles Babbage, a mathematician who had designed the first programmable computer, called the Analytical Engine. Lovelace designed a method of programming punched cards so the engine could have performed useful—and difficult—calculations. However, the engine needed 8,000 precisely made parts. That made it so expensive that it was never actually built.

Programs stored in punched cards were also used by the US inventor Herman Hollerith to program a powerful electrical calculating machine. Calculations used to be called computations, so Hollerith's machine was called a computer. The US government used Hollerith's machine to count its citizens in the 1890 national **census**. Hollerith's computer company went on to be called International Business Machines, or IBM. IBM is now one of the largest technology companies in the world. It has been developing robots and AI for 40 years.

This computer was designed by Herman Hollerith in 1884.

CHAPTER 2

DECISION-MAKING

A robot that can function like a human being has to make a lot of decisions, such as when and how to move, when to speak, and what to say. Humans make these kinds of decisions all the time, often without thinking. For robots, making a decision is not the same thing as thinking. In order to work, robots do not need to think—at least, not in the sense of the word we apply to people. Whether AI robots can think, or will be able to think in the future, is a complex question—but the drink dispenser at your local burger joint, the robots in a car factory, and the speech-enabled robot assistants on your smartphone or tablet are not thinking. Instead, they are making decisions using mathematics.

Any computer input has to be coded using only two digits, 1 and 0.

A **microchip** at the heart of any computer makes millions of yes-or-no decisions every second.

Finding the answer (or output) to a question (or input) requires **logic**. The mathematics of logic is called Boolean **algebra**. It was named for George Boole, the Englishman who came up with it in the 1850s. Boolean algebra is a little odd. It only deals with two numbers, 1 and 0. There is no such thing as 2 or above. The answer to any sum, even 1+1, must be either 1 or 0.

Boolean math puts the "digit" into digital. Digital technology gets its name because it works using numbers, or digits: 1s and 0s. Computer programs are written in languages that use a code made up of words, symbols, and numbers, but these codes are later compiled into strings of 1s and 0s called the machine code. A digital device, such as the microchip that controls a drink dispenser or an unmanned aircraft, runs on machine code.

Each microchip is filled with a billion or more tiny components called **transistors**. A transistor is essentially a switch made of silicon and other chemicals that can turn an electric current on or off millions of times a second. A 1 in the code might switch it on, and a 0 switch it off again. Every decision a robot makes is due to the work of these switches in converting an input of machine code into an output.

USING LOGIC

A computer processor is a programmable device. It does not have preset instructions. Instead, it can run any list of instructions it is given. The processor components that carry out the instructions in the order specified are called logic gates. Generally these are clusters of transistors and semiconductors that are hardwired into a particular configuration.

Processors are part of complex electronic circuits.

Each logic gate can carry out a specific type of Boolean mathematics. These are not the usual mathematical operations of adding, subtracting, and multiplying. Instead, Boolean algebra uses a set of operations that includes, for example, AND, OR, and NOT. All the possible outcomes of each operation make up what is called a truth table. These charts resemble multiplication tables—but only ever use 1s and 0s.

BEHIND THE THEORY

George Boole was originally from England but moved to teach math at the university in Cork, Ireland. In 1854, Boole set out his way of using math to make logical decisions in a book entitled *The Laws of Thought*. Ten years later, Boole caught pneumonia after being caught out in a heavy rainstorm. His wife, Mary, believed the best course of action was to treat an illness with whatever caused it, so she poured buckets of water over him. George was dead within two weeks.

The father of modern computer code died after being caught out in the rain.

In the AND operation, two inputs come into a logic gate. If both the inputs are 1 AND 1, the gate outputs a 1. That means it allows an electric current to flow out to the next gate in the sequence. If one of the inputs is a 0, the output is always 0, so the current is turned off. An OR gate outputs a 1 whether the inputs are 1 OR 0. It only outputs a 0—stopping the current—if both inputs are 0. A NOT gate outputs whatever the input is NOT: a 0 becomes a 1 and a 1 becomes a 0.

At the most basic level, all computer activity is controlled by logic gates that apply these simple rules. If humans are to use computers to make a robot as intelligent as we are, we would first need to break intelligence down into a sequence of millions of logical steps. No one knows if that is possible.

-CHAPTER 3-

ARTIFICIAL INTELLIGENCE

Many experts predict that artificial intelligence will change the world—for better or for worse. However, the things AI will do in the future, and even how it operates now, may not be what you are expecting. In fact, it can be misleading to talk about AI as if it is a "thing" that a robot or computer system possesses. Instead it is probably more accurate and useful to say that a robot is an artificial intelligence, or an AI. This is because there are many different types of AIs, which have been given intelligence using a range of different techniques.

A newborn baby has no knowledge of the behavior required to function as a regular human being.

How do you even start to make a machine that is intelligent? Programming an entire brain's worth of intelligence into a robot does not seem possible. Instead, computer scientists and robot engineers are trying to create machines that can copy the way that humans—and other animals—developed our own intelligence.

Despite what your mother might have told you, when you were born, you could not do much. A newborn human baby cannot sit, stand, talk, or even see clearly. All it can really do is breathe, suck, cry, and poop.

A newborn baby quickly begins to develop mentally and physically. Within a couple of years the baby will have learned a great many things—and its intelligence will only increase further through education. (That's what school is for!)

The best way to make a robot intelligent is to teach it stuff. In 1948, a US-born British brain scientist named William Grey Walter decided to use robots to investigate how brains learned. His devices looked like turtles. They had domed bodies, three wheels so they could turn on the spot, and light sensors. Grey Walter found that Elmer and Elsie, as he named his robots, could learn how to move in complex ways using a simple computer brain. They could even demonstrate behavior which, in an animal such as a rat or ant, might be described as "fear" or "curiosity." The robots stopped these behaviors once their controller was erased—and then they learned new ones. Not only did Elmer and Elsie show how a simple brain could learn complex things, they also revealed how we could build machines that could learn to be smart.

Children can learn many things—including how to program their own robots.

NEURAL NETWORKS

A regular computer can do many remarkable things. It can add funny filters to photos, it can play chess with you, and it can tell you how to navigate through a city far from home. However, it does all these things by following a program. It cannot learn to do something for which it has no instructions. An AI is able to change its programming by itself, so it can either learn a new task or, more likely, learn to do a preprogrammed task better. It does this with a computer circuit called a neural network.

A neural network (or net for short) is made up of layers. It has at least four layers, but the more it has, the smarter it will be. The first layer receives inputs, which are raw data for the net to learn about. The final layer has the outputs, which are essentially all the different possible conclusions the neural net draws from the inputs. The layers in between are described as hidden.

A new neural net is set a task, such as learning to recognize a picture of a cat. The inputs are the **pixels** of a picture of a cat.

A neural net tries to achieve the same results as a human brain, but works in a completely different way.

A neural net learns how to recognize a cat by studying millions of images of cats.

The characteristics of every pixel—its position, brightness, color—are passed to every component in the first hidden layer of the net. These components, or classifiers, evaluate the chance that a pixel is from a cat or not. They send their results to the classifiers in the next layer, weighting each signal according to the chances of the pixel being from a cat or not. Eventually, the final layer of the net will output an answer: cat. At first, the net will be wrong as much as it is right. But it does the test many millions of times over—it works fast—and is told each time if it is wrong or right. Gradually it learns which route "cat" data takes through the net, and eventually it knows that any new data taking that route is a cat. Smart.

UNANSWERED

Neural means "belonging to the nervous system," and the idea for a neural network was to make a microchip that worked like a brain. However, a neural net learns in a different way from an animal's brain. In animals, nerve cells, or neurons, communicate using pulses of electricity and chemical messengers. Learning creates networks of cells that store information. However, nerve signals vary in frequency and intensity, and no one has discovered how to decode their activity into information.

TYPES OF AI

AI technology is already at work in everyday life. Predictive text which figures out what you want to say as you type is AI. Recommendations for songs to listen to and products to buy online all use AI. However, the AI that does these things could not hold a conversation, be your friend or pet—or really "know" anything at all.

The AI in your phone can answer questions but not chat with you.

There are several ways of describing an AI. These examples are all what are termed narrow AIs. A narrow AI has been programmed to learn one thing. The voice-activated assistants that listen to our requests and answer our questions are another type of narrow AI. They were taught to understand speech by computer scientists—and over time, they will get better at it as they listen and respond to millions of users all over the world. (The AI is not inside the individual device, but on a main computer connected to the Internet.) The assistant does not really have a list of questions that it knows the answer to, either. Its designers have added a few examples, and the software AI interprets what you actually want. (It might not always get it right, but it will learn.)

An AI that learns millions of legal cases will be as skilled as any human lawyer.

Another form of AI is called an expert system. This is essentially a **database** filled with knowledge that would ordinarily be in the head of a human expert, such as a doctor or a lawyer. The expert system makes decisions based on this large store of knowledge. For example, a patient can input their medical symptoms, and the expert AI will give the patient a **diagnosis**.

Combining expert systems with narrow AI that can learn makes a system even smarter. It is already often true that such systems can outsmart humans. However, these systems can only outsmart humans in one field. A human can switch to another task, while the AI cannot.

UNANSWERED

An AI that is as intelligent as a human—or even smarter—is described as a strong AI. Strong AI does not yet exist, and no one knows if it will ever be possible. The difference between narrow AI (also known as weak AI) and strong AI is that the strong AI would be able to direct its own learning abilities to different tasks. It would be able to figure out what it needs to know and then learn it—just like humans.

BIG DATA

People can already control home systems such as their heating remotely using phones or tablets.

The Internet is a network of computer networks. When it was created, it connected the large networks of computers used by universities, government organizations, and companies. Then scientists used the telephone system to connect home computers to the Internet. Next came smartphones, tablets, TVs, watches, and game consoles. What next?

The answer is that just about anything will be connected to the Internet in the future: refrigerators, central heating, stoplights, trains, cars, greenhouses, and even toilets. People are connecting these devices to the Internet so they can turn them on and off by remote control and monitor what they are doing. However, the process may also have a hidden benefit for the development of AI.

The first wave of the Internet can be seen as being about connecting large organizations so they could share data. In the next wave, individuals used it to communicate. The next wave is being called the Internet of Things. There are already more devices connected to the Internet than there are people on Earth, and the number is set to rise. All these "things" will be sending and receiving information—in huge quantities. Computer scientists call this information Big Data.

UNANSWERED

Humans are conscious, meaning we are aware of our existence—and also aware that there are other consciousnesses that are aware of different things. No one knows how we are conscious. It is a mystery about the brain. One theory is that consciousness arises from the complexity and quantity of our brains' activity. If so, then mixing Big Data with AI might have the same result. It might create a conscious machine. But how would we know?

Big Data is made up of billions of bits of information: traffic flow on the highway, the power level in the electricity network, the amount of water being used in washing machines in Texas. Each single fact seems dull, but taken all together, Big Data could be very useful in planning how to manage water, power, transportation, and other essential services. Humans are smart enough to come up with the idea of Big Data, but not smart enough to understand it. Only AIs can process all that information and make sense of it. Now imagine an AI that is learning from all the other AIs. You have a smart, expert machine that can run an entire city!

The movement of individual cars along the highway adds to Big Data.

-CHAPTER 4-

TESTING AI

A computer can be very smart compared to a human. For example, it could multiply 1,345,689,752,528,394 by 346,225,289 faster than a human could even read the question. However, is that the same as being intelligent?

Computers are outstanding at math, but that does not mean they can actually think.

The twentieth-century British mathematician Alan Turing was one of the founders of computing. In 1950, he developed a simple test for judging whether a robot or any other computer-driven system was "intelligent." The only requirement was that the AI needed to be able to hold a conversation. Even the most intelligent AI would fail what is known as the Turing Test if it could not speak or type out text (although if it really were intelligent, it should be able figure out a way to do so).

The Turing Test is set up like this. A human judge is alone in a room. They converse with two test subjects hidden from view in two other rooms. One of the subjects is the AI being tested. The other is a human. The judge has no idea which is which or who is who. To make it more fair, the conversation is through written text, because an AI might not be able to speak very well.

The judge holds a conversation with the two hidden subjects and reads their responses to the statements or questions. The test finishes when the human judge decides which subject is human and which is the computer. If the judge gets it wrong, then the AI is judged intelligent.

Given enough time to make a considered decision, no human judge has ever been fooled into believing a computer program is intelligent. However, in short tests—limited to around five minutes each—conversation software known as chatbots have come close.

The chatbots take advantage of weaknesses in the Turing Test. For example, humans make mistakes while they type, so chatbots are programmed to make mistakes, too. There are other problems with the test, but it is a useful starting point to understand what AI—and other kinds of intelligence—really is.

Alan Turing developed a computer to break German codes in World War II (1939–1945).

THE CHINESE ROOM

劇場

A human can copy out Chinese characters without knowing any Chinese.

Imagine an AI that has passed the Turing test. It does not have a living brain and nervous system, but whatever method it uses makes it appear just as intelligent as a human. That would mean the AI thinks, and even feels, like a human. It has an artificial mind. Alan Turing would have agreed. He thought it did not matter how an AI worked. As long as it appeared to think, it should be treated as a thinking being with a mind. However, an American philosopher named John Searle disagreed. To support his view, he came up with a version of the Turing Test called the Chinese Room in 1980.

In the Chinese Room, the AI has been replaced by a human, who is hidden away inside a locked room. The human judge speaks only Chinese. They write all their questions in Chinese characters and send them into the room. The person inside the room cannot speak or read Chinese. They have a list of Chinese characters so they can decipher each message. They also have a list of answers in Chinese for each possible question. They copy their answer out in Chinese and send it back for the judge to read. The judge cannot tell if the answers are from an AI or a Chinese-speaking human. In fact, they are from neither.

It is not possible to know if people see the same colors when they look at the same objects.

UNANSWERED

In the same way that we might not know if a computer is conscious, there is no test to show that another person is conscious. They may act just as you do, but you cannot know whether their awareness of the world matches your own. Consciousness involves internal experiences called qualia, which are things such as color, smell, and taste. How can you know that your color qualia match those of your friend? You both see a blue sky and a green tree, but their blue qualia may actually be your green one, and their green qualia your blue.

Searle wanted to show that the human in the Chinese Room is working in the same way an AI works. An AI might have programming that can fool a judge into thinking it is human, but the AI—like the hidden human in the Chinese Room—has no awareness of what is being said. Even the best AIs would function unconsciously, so Searle believes it is impossible to compare their abilities with our own.

John Searle is a leading philosopher thinking about issues related to AI and robots.

PLAYING GAMES

One of the best ways to develop AI is to make computers that play games. Games such as tic-tac-toe, checkers, and backgammon are based on strategy. There is a best move in any situation. Computers can solve all the possible outcomes of every move—and should always win.

Chess is a complex strategy game. The number of possible combinations of moves adds up to a 10 followed by 120 zeros—more than any computer can process. However, in 1997 an IBM chess computer named Deep Blue defeated the reigning chess world champion, Russian Garry Kasparov—but only just. Deep Blue was an expert AI. It learned the moves in 700,000 games by expert players. As it played, Deep Blue used this database to figure out what to do next.

The first computer programs for playing chess were written in the early 1950s.

BEHIND THE THEORY

Alan Turing, one of the world's first computer scientists, began his career as a mathematician. In 1936, he dreamed up a theoretical device called the Turing Machine. The machine could follow any coded **algorithm**. Turing intended the machine to be a system for understanding the limits of mathematics. Instead, it became the model for the first digital computers.

Deep Blue sometimes made mistakes, but these odd moves disturbed Kasparov. He was worried the machine could see something he could not—and that led him to make mistakes.

IBM also built Watson, an AI that could understand spoken questions. In 2011 Watson appeared on the *Jeopardy* quiz show, and beat all the human contestants. (It was very good at the answers, but was also able to press its buzzer faster than its opponents.)

Perhaps the smartest computer yet built is AlphaGo. In 2016, it beat the world champion at Go, a Chinese game even more complex than chess. There are more possible moves than there are atoms in the universe.

Watson had two advantages on *Jeopardy*: knowledge and speed.

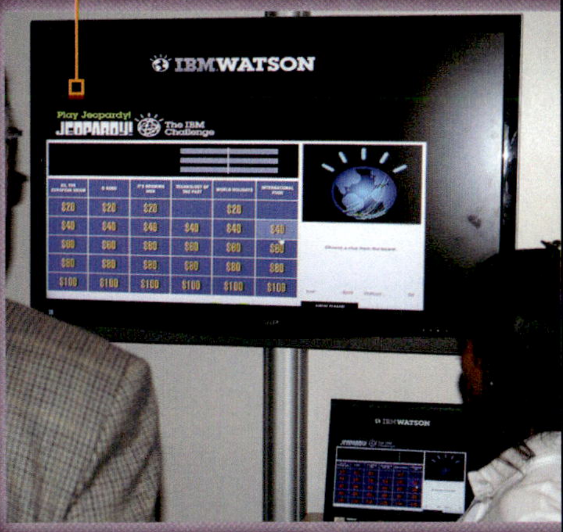

-CHAPTER 5-

THE ROBOTS ARE COMING

The world is on the edge of a revolution in robotics. Many of the jobs now done by human workers will one day be done by robots. For some this is an exciting prospect—it will mean they can leave work to the machines and have more time for fun. For others, the rise of the robots is a real worry. Machines could put them out of a job—or even take over!

Neither of these visions of the future may play out as people expect. To explore the potential results of a robot revolution, we have to compare a robot and a human worker. Robots can do three things better than a human. First, robots never get bored or tired. They can repeat the same job over and over with the same movements. This is ideal for manufacturing work.

A **drone** can fly a programmed route or can be controlled remotely by a pilot.

Robots are unlikely to be able to carry out repairs to infrastructure.

Second, robots can go to places that are too dangerous for humans. For example, drones—technically called unmanned aerial vehicles, or UAVs—already fly over battlefields carrying cameras or weapons. The police use robots to investigate suspected bombs. It is also safer (and cheaper) to send robots to explore other planets than human astronauts.

The third way robots outperform humans is in the application of knowledge. A robot, or more likely a computer-based "bot," is very good at analyzing data and reaching a conclusion based on its expert database. For example, a bot could diagnose a patient based on test and scan results more accurately than a human doctor. It could advise people about legal procedures more reliably than a lawyer using its database of past cases. Or it could manage business and finance by analyzing market data more quickly than a human analyst.

By contrast, manual work is tough for robots to do. Cleaning the streets, delivering parcels, and fixing leaking pipes require coordinating many actions at once. So if the robot revolution is going to replace human workers, it is very likely it will put experts such as doctors, lawyers, and bankers out of business, not workers such as cleaners, nurses, and builders.

ON THE ROAD

One of the first noticeable changes in the robot revolution is likely to be on the roads. At the moment, driverless cars look the same as regular cars, except the steering wheel, gears, and control pedals are moved automatically by robotics. This is similar to what happened with the first automobiles. They used the design of horse-drawn carriages before they evolved into modern cars. Driverless cars will evolve, too. They have no need for a driver's seat, for example, so that will disappear in the future.

Many cars are already equipped with satellite navigation (sat-nav) systems.

The important part of a driverless car is not really the robotics that control steering and speed. It is the computer that does the driving. The computers in the driverless cars being tested today use four systems to figure out where they are, where they are going—and when to go and when to stop!

UNANSWERED

In the United States today, most families have their own car. When cars become driverless, will people still need to own cars? Car-sharing apps would allow people to hire the nearest robot car for each journey. These cars might be owned by a company, or could work for themselves. Their AI controls would allow them to move to new locations to find more work and to set their own prices. The car's profits will be used for maintenance and upgrades.

The first is not that revolutionary: **Global Positioning System (GPS)** technology is already used by sat-nav systems. GPS data tells the car where it is and gives it information about speed limits, stoplights, and junctions on the planned journey.

Next, the car uses cameras to get an all-around picture of its surroundings. The computer uses the camera to "see" road markings and objects around the car. A **radar** system also scans around the car. This detects the exact distance of every object and its speed in relation to the car. The final sensor is called LiDar. Instead of using radio waves like a radar, this system scans the surroundings with an invisible **laser**. LiDar data allows the car to differentiate nearby objects into cars, pedestrians, and road signs. Now that it knows all that, it just drives!

This illustration shows how driverless cars use sensors to "see" the road.

IN THE FACTORY

Robots have been at work on assembly lines for the last 50 years. Modern cars—whether they are driverless or not—are mainly built by robots. Robots lift, screw, weld, and paint components, overseen by a few human workers.

A van body on an assembly line moves past robot arms that add new components.

The most familiar industrial robots are robot arms. They work on assembly lines, where each arm performs particular tasks. These arms have as many as 10 joints, making them highly mobile. The joints give the arm up to six degrees of freedom, meaning that it can move in six independent motions, allowing it to twist, lever, and extend. The human arm is more mobile than a robot arm. It has seven degrees of freedom. However, the robotic alternatives are much stronger, never need a rest as they repeat the same task 24 hours a day, and can be programmed to move with much greater precision than a human hand.

BEHIND THE THEORY

The first assembly robot was the Unimate, which went into service in car factories in the 1960s. The robotic arm's job was to pick up metal components and weld them to the body of the car—a dangerous job for a human worker. Unimate was invented by the American George Devol. Devol invented many other things, such as the Speedy Weeny, an automatic hot dog oven that dispensed food to hungry commuters. Another of Devol's innovations is the automatic door that slides open when a person breaks a light beam as they approach.

A scientist programs Unimate in 1961.

A robot arm is based on an invention called the stepper motor. This electrical motor uses magnets to rotate a metallic cog. The magnets apply a precise force for a precise time, so the stepper motor can make very small and exact movements.

Assembly robots are often built for a specific production process, but an articulated robot arm can be taught different jobs. The precise movements of the arm through space can be preprogrammed by a human user. This is the most precise method of setting up a robot arm, but it is very time consuming. A faster method is called "leading by the nose," in which a human teacher moves the robot through the required sequence of motions. The robot remembers the motions, then repeats them automatically.

SMART HOMES

Robots and AI will appear in your home soon—if they are not there already. They will create "smart" homes that run automatically and figure out what its residents need without them thinking about it.

Technology of all kinds has changed enormously in the last century. Oddly, however, the places where we live—our homes—have not changed very much during that time, despite innovations such as television, air conditioning, and computers. A time traveler from the 1900s would not find a modern home all that different from what they were used to. The home still has familiar elements: beds, chairs, tables, doors, and windows.

When homes are truly smart, we will no longer need phones to control them.

Now it's your turn to travel into the future—not too far. This future will still be familiar but much smarter. There is no need to use a key. The front door simply recognizes your voice and opens when you ask it. It also knows if you are expecting visitors or deliveries. The door knows all your messages telling you if something is being delivered, and it has heard your telephone calls, so it can recognize your friends' voices when they turn up.

UNANSWERED

At its most efficient, a smart house will have to analyze data from many sources—your diary, your phone calls, the weather outside, your heart rate, your tone of voice, and even your feces. That information is shared as it is added to Big Data from millions of other homes. That is how your house will learn to make the best decisions for you—but how would you feel about every bit of your life being shared as information in this way?

You enter the house after a hard day at work. Your fitness tracker has told the house how busy or stressed you have been. Music is playing to suit your mood, and curtains close automatically. The weather forecast tells the house that it will be a cold night, so the heating is gradually warming the living room and bathroom. The kitchen is preparing a meal; the house knows what you like to eat from what you take from the fridge. The fridge buys food automatically so it never runs out. Your toilet monitors your waste for missing nutrients or signs of illness (in a serious case, the robot toilet would call the doctor). The house senses your presence as you move around and switches lights on or off. You can change any of its decisions—meal time, temperature, music—simply by asking. Sounds pretty smart!

A smart fridge will record what you use—and order more to be delivered.

-CHAPTER 6-

ROBOTS AND AI IN THE FUTURE

Robotics and AI are not necessarily turning out like they appear in science-fiction movies. We use robots for many applications, but they do not look like the androids played by actors and actresses. Instead they may take the form of self-flying drones, exploration rovers on Mars, robot arms in factories, and voice-activated assistants on every computer. At the same time, AI is filtering our Internet searches to get the best hits, buying and selling our investments in lightning-fast trades, and checking medical scans for problems. However, unlike in science fiction, robots are not our friends, they do not look like us, and they are nowhere near as intelligent. Will the super-smart androids of science fiction ever become fact?

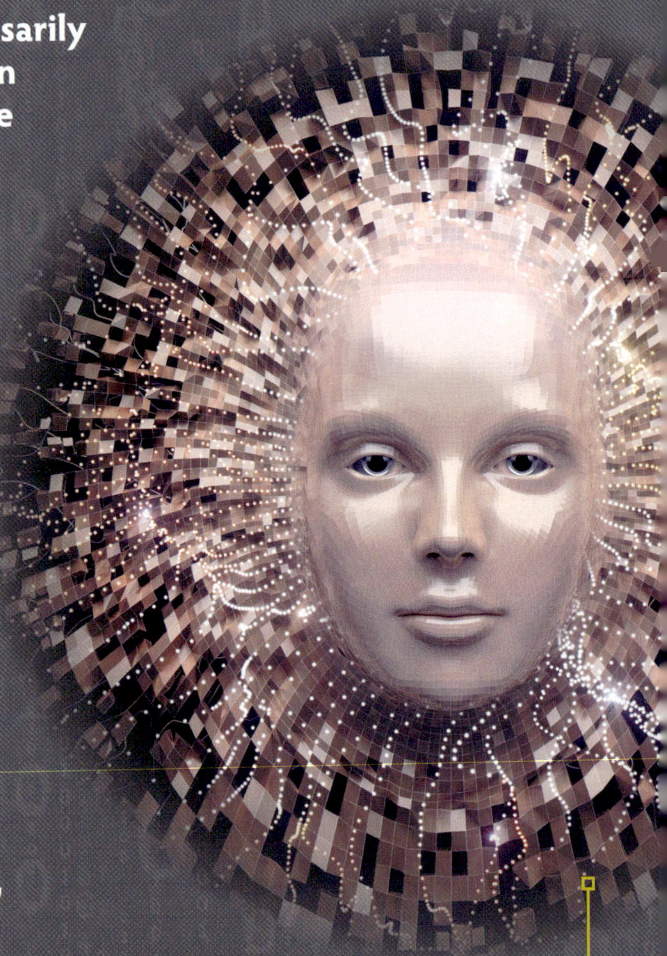

One of the challenges facing engineers is to make robots whose faces look like those of real humans.

The latest attempt to make a robot human is the actroid—an android that acts like a human. Most of the work has gone into developing an actroid's face that is a realistic copy of a human face (often that of a real person). The actroid has soft, fleshy skin, blinks its eyes, and moves its mouth as it talks. In a major technological advance, the actroid's camera eyes detect the expression of the human it is talking to and understands the human's mood. In response, the actroid chooses its facial expressions—happy, angry, or frightened—to match the mood of the conversation.

The faces and bodies of actroids are becoming increasingly realistic copies of humans. However, actroids still fall into what is sometimes known as the "uncanny valley." People feel uneasy or even revolted by the presence of the machines, which are close to being human but are not quite right. We find a waddling metal robot with flashing lights much more endearing than an actroid that looks and behaves like a close copy of us. Perhaps people will get used to actroids—but perhaps they make people nervous for good reason!

Androids are easily told apart from humans. If scientists are successful at producing actroids, that might no longer be true.

ARE HUMANS IN DANGER FROM AI?

People have worried about robots and AI from the moment writers and scientists started thinking about them. Today, it is clear that there are limits and dangers associated with AI.

One problem is that AI is easy to fool. A narrow AI such as a driverless car relies on sensors, but it is relatively easy to trick them. For example, a camera cannot tell the difference between a real road and a picture of a road. Small changes to a road sign could confuse the car, which might make a driving error as a result. This is due to how AI learns. It is very good at analyzing the bits of data that make up the shape of a road sign or pedestrian, but it does not have a larger concept of "sign" or "pedestrian" like a human does.

Another big problem with AI is more sinister. It might be very good at its job—and sometimes that job is to kill. Robots are being developed by the military for different jobs. Human soldiers are being fitted with robotic **exoskeletons** so they can run faster and carry more without getting tired.

Atlas is a two-legged android designed to carry loads on the battlefield.

BEHIND THE THEORY

Elon Musk is a South African computer scientist and engineer. His Tesla cars were the first road vehicles to have a self-driving autopilot mode. However, in 2017, Musk warned that AI technology could be dangerous. He pointed out that governments set rules to ensure safety for things like cars, medicines, and construction, and said they should be doing the same for AI. If they do not, Musk warned, "In the end, the machines will win."

The same idea is also helping paralyzed people. Four-legged robots, such as BigDog, are designed to carry heavy loads in rough terrain. BigDog was discontinued for being too noisy, but strong two-legged androids, such as Atlas, may take its place. One day entire armies will be made from robotic weapon systems. Human armies prefer not to fight to avoid loss of human life. If an army is made up of nonhuman robots, would commanders be more likely to send it into battle?

Would armies of robot warriors save human lives—or cost more?

QUANTUM COMPUTING

If humans are ever going to fit an intelligent computer brain into a robot, we will need a new kind of computer. The best chance of that is what is known as a quantum computer.

The most powerful supercomputers are able to process more data, more quickly, than the human brain. However, the programs they use are not capable of matching the function of the human brain. Even if we could figure out a program that could function in the same way as the brain, a powerful enough supercomputer would still fill a large building and need its own power plant. In contrast, the human brain in your head uses less power than a big light bulb.

An ordinary computer handles data in small pieces called bits. A bit can only ever be one of two states: 1 or 0, or on or off. A 32-bit computer handles strings of 32 bits at a time. Supercomputers can handle larger chunks of information, but the process is the same.

The race is on to develop devices with more processing power than classical computers.

BEHIND THE THEORY

The technology company Google is at the forefront of computer development. With NASA, it has developed the largest quantum computer, D-Wave. D-Wave has just 1,000 quantum bits, but it is 100 million times more powerful than a classical microchip of that size. D-Wave is being used to tackle mathematics that would take a classical computer centuries to solve. Google hopes D-Wave's processing power will show a new way to solve hard puzzles.

D-Wave is the first attempt to put quantum computing into practice.

Instead of the on–off electronics of a classical computer, a quantum computer would hold data in a form called quantum bits or qubits using the characteristic states of atoms. For example, if atoms are spinning up, that would represent 1, while spinning down would represent 0. However, due to the weirdness of **quantum physics**, an atom can spin up and down at the same time, so it can be a 1 or 0 at the same time. So 1 qubit holds 2 bits of information; 2 qubits hold 4 bits; 5 qubits have 32 bits—and 32 qubits hold 4,294,967,296 bits!

That is the power of quantum computing—in theory. In practice, quantum computers are still in their infancy. They only work in vacuums that are shielded from Earth's magnetism and are colder than outer space. For AI robots to become a reality, this cutting-edge technology will have to advance rapidly—just as robotics and AI have advanced rapidly in the last 100 years.

TIMELINE

1495	Italian artist and inventor Leonardo da Vinci designs a metal man operated by gears.
1700s	Mechanical automata are popular in Europe.
1804	In France, fabric merchant Joseph Marie Charles uses punched hole cards to program a loom.
1840s	Ada Lovelace writes programs for the Analytical Engine invented by Charles Babbage. However, the machine is never built.
1854	English mathematician George Boole writes *The Laws of Thought*, outlining the principles of Boolean algebra.
1884	US inventor Herman Hollerith invents a calculating machine or computer programmed using punched cards.
1890	Hollerith's computer is used to tally the results of the US census.
1900	The novel *The Wizard of Oz* introduces a robotlike character named the Tin Man.
1921	Czech writer Karel Capek coins the word "robot" for humanlike machines.
1928	British manufacturers create an android named Erik.
1942	Science-fiction writer Isaac Asimov introduces his Three Laws of Robotics.

1948 Scientist William Grey Walter builds Elmer and Elsie to test robots' ability to learn.

1950 British mathematician Alan Turing devises the Turing Test for judging whether a machine is "intelligent."

1961 Unimate, a robot arm invented by George Devol, begins work on car assembly lines in the United States.

1980 US philosopher John Searle proposes the Chinese Room, a model that suggests the limitations of AI.

1997 The chess computer Deep Blue defeats reigning world chess champion Garry Kasparov.

2011 The IBM computer Watson appears on the TV show *Jeopardy*.

2011 D-Wave One, the world's first commercially available quantum computer, goes on sale.

2015 An improved D-Wave quantum computer is released with 1,000+ qubits.

2016 The computer AlphaGo defeats the world champion at the Chinese game of Go.

2017 Technology pioneer Elon Musk warns of the potential dangers the development of AI poses to the human race.

GLOSSARY

algebra a type of mathematics that uses letters and symbols to solve equations

algorithm a set of rules a computer follows to solve a problem

artificial intelligence computer systems that can perform tasks that usually involve human intelligence

assembly lines series of workers or machines in a factory that assemble a product as it passes along

automata mechanical devices that can perform repeated tasks

automate to convert a process so it is performed mainly by machines

census an official count of a population

components individual parts that are put together to create a machine

database a collection of information stored so it is easily accessible

diagnosis the identification of an illness from the symptoms of a patient

drone an unmanned aerial vehicle (UAV), or pilotless aircraft

effectors parts of a robot that respond to a stimulus, or input

electromechanical relating to a mechanical device that is operated by electricity

exoskeletons external frameworks that support a body

Global Positioning System (GPS) a system that uses satellites to precisely pinpoint locations on Earth

hardware the physical parts of a computer

laser a narrow beam of highly concentrated light

logic a system of reasoning based on small, provable steps

loom a machine for weaving thread into cloth

mechanical performed by a machine

microchip a tiny wafer of material that contains electrical cricuits

philosopher someone who thinks about profound questions of existence

pixels tiny pieces of illumination that create an electrical or digital image

processors the parts of a computer or robot that process information

programmed given a set of instructions to perform a task

quantum physics the behavior of atoms and subatomic particles

radar a device that bounces radio waves off objects to locate them

radio the transmission of invisible electromagnetic waves

semiconductors devices that conduct a limited amount of electricity

sensors devices that detect something physical, such as light or heat

strategy a plan to achieve overall success

transistors devices that alter the flow of electricity

FOR MORE INFORMATION

BOOKS

Cunningham, Anne C. *Artificial Intelligence and the Technological Singularity.* New York, NY: Greenhaven Publishing, 2017.

Doeden, Matt. *Can You Survive an Artificial Intelligence Uprising? An Interactive Doomsday Adventure.* North Mankato, MN: Capstone Press, 2016.

Martin, Claudia. *Robotics in Industry.* New York, NY: Lucent Books, 2018.

McPherson, Stephanie Sammartino. *Artificial Intelligence: Building Smarter Machines.* Minneapolis, MN: Twenty-First Century Books, 2018.

Ogden, Charlie. *Surviving a Robot Revolution.* New York: Gareth Stevens Publishing, 2018.

WEBSITES

www.kidscodecs.com/what-is-artificial-intelligence
An article about AI from the kids' online computer magazine *beanz.*

science.howstuffworks.com/robot.htm
Pages from How Stuff Works about robots and their history, and the future of artificial intelligence.

kids.nationalgeographic.com/explore/youtube-playlist-pages/youtube-playlist-robots
National Geographic has compiled a playlist of robot videos on YouTube.

www.industrytap.com/brief-history-robots/29235
A timeline of the history of robotics.

Publisher's note to educators and parents: Our editors have carefully reviewed these websites to ensure that they are suitable for students. Many websites change frequently, however, and we cannot guarantee that a site's future contents will continue to meet our high standards of quality and educational value. Be advised that students should be closely supervised whenever they access the Internet.

INDEX